bake me I'm yours...
cookie

Lindy Smith

David and Charles

A DAVID & CHARLES BOOK
Copyright © David & Charles Limited
2008, 2010

David & Charles is an F+W Media Inc. company
4700 East Galbraith Road
Cincinnati, OH 45236

First published in 2008
This paperback edition first published in the UK
in 2010
Reprinted 2010 (twice)

Text and designs copyright © Lindy Smith
2008, 2010
Photography copyright © David & Charles
2008, 2010

A catalogue record for this book is available
from the British Library.

ISBN-13: 978-0-7153-3763-9 paperback
ISBN-10: 0-7153-3763-7 paperback

Printed in China by Toppan Leefung
Printing Limited
for David & Charles
Brunel House   Newton Abbot   Devon

Commissioning Editor: Jennifer Fox-Proverbs
Desk Editor: Emily Rae
Text Editor: Bethany Dymond
Art Editor: Sarah Underhill
Designer: Emma Sandquest
Production Controller: Kelly Smith
Photographer: Kim Sayer

David & Charles publish high quality books on a
wide range of subjects.
For more great book ideas visit: **www.rucraft.co.uk**

contents

cookie heaven…

Cookies – serve them with coffee, hang them from your Christmas tree or place them in clear cookie bags or decorative boxes and give to your friends and family. There are always plenty of reasons for you to have fun creating your own little works of art.

Cookies are delicious in their own right, of course, but adding decoration makes them that extra bit special. Many of the cookies included in this book can be decorated in a couple of minutes, but by spending a little more time you can create cookies that are truly magical and almost too good to eat.

Fundamentally a designer at heart, I have thoroughly enjoyed putting this little book of cookies together. With a background in sugarcraft, I have found that cookies, like cakes, make an excellent canvas on which to create designs that are both appealing and stylish.

I have included as many techniques and types of icing as possible, although I must admit to favouring decorating cookies using sugarpaste. With sugarpaste you can not only easily introduce colour but also add texture and three-dimensional elements to create cookies that will wow all those who see them.

As you probably appreciate, decorating cookies is child's play; cookies are all about having fun in your kitchen and creating gorgeous, tasty treats that everyone will love. I have included a range of ideas in this book to tempt you, from high fashion to seasonal delights, weddings to designer style, so that whatever the occasion, you'll be able to treat your friends, lighten up your work colleague's day or spoil your family.

When it comes to decorating cookies, the possibilities really are endless so I hope that you will be inspired not only to create cookies from this book but also to invent designs of your own. If you can't find a cutter for the type of cookie you would like to make, then do not despair – simply make your own templates, as described on page 11.

Be inspired, be creative and most of all, have fun.

Lindy

www.lindyscakes.co.uk

basic tools & equipment

Before you begin to bake your cookies you will need to ensure that you have all of the right tools for the job to hand. The following is a list of equipment that have been used frequently in the book, although you will find that a wide range of sugarcrafting tools are suitable. Suppliers (in brackets) can be found on p120.

⊛ **Baking sheets** (1) for baking cookies

⊛ **Craft knife** (2) for intricate cutting tasks

⊛ **Cutters** (3) for embossing and cutting out paste. I used

  * circle cutters (FMM)

  * paisley, small teardrop, heart, scalloped diamond (LC)

  * flat floral collection (LC)

  * stars (LC)

  * indian scrolls (LC)

  * patchwork cutters (PC)

  * handbag cutters (LC)

⊛ **Moulds** (4) for creating flower centres. I used daisy centre stamps (JEM)

⊛ **Paintbrushes** (5) a range of sizes used for stippling, painting and dusting

⊛ **Paint palette**, for mixing paste colours and dusts prior to painting

⊛ **Palette knife** (6) for cutting paste

⊛ **Piping tubes** (7) for piping royal icing and cutting out small circles

⊛ **Disposable piping bag** (8)

⊛ **Coupler for reusable piping bag** (8a) The coupler is connected to the bag, which holds the royal icing whilst piping, and allows the tube to be changed easily

⊛ **Rolling pin** (9) for rolling out different types of paste

⊛ **Stick embossers** (10) for adding patterns to paste (HP)

⊛ **Sugar shaper and disc** (11) for creating pieces of uniformly shaped modelling paste

⊛ **Tools**

  * ball tool (FMM), makes even indentations in paste and softens the edges of petals (12)

  * dresden tool (FMM), to create marking on paste (13)

  * cutting wheel (PME), used instead of a knife to avoid dragging the paste (14)

  * quilting tool (PME), used to add stitching lines to paste (15)

⊛ **Wire cooling rack** (16) for allowing cookies to cool after baking

⊛ **Work board** (17) non-stick, used for rolling out pastes

making shapes

It's never been simpler to transform an ordinary cookie into a work of art! There are a variety of cutters on the market in every imaginable shape and size, from simple gingerbread men to stylish handbags. If you can't find the cutter you are searching for, it is easy to create a template to work from – simply follow the advice given here.

cookie cutters

Whether you want a classic gingerbread man or luscious lips, you will be spoilt for choice by the range of cutters available. For cheap and cheerful cutters that do the job, choose from an array of mass-produced, colourful plastic cutters. Tinplate cutters are also low cost but have to be cared for as they are prone to rust. Handcrafted copper and stainless steel cutters are more of an investment but they are strong, safe and hold their shape after years of repeated use. Stainless steel cutters are even dishwasher friendly!

Many cutters have a rounded lip or top edge which makes them easier to hold. However, cutters without this lip are reversible, which means that they are much more versatile for a-symmetrical shapes, such as the Wonky Wonder cookies (p36).

templates

If you just can't find a suitable cutter, one option to consider is making and using a template instead. Find an image that appeals to you and resize it using a computer or photocopier. Size is very much a personal choice and dependent on the shape of the image; try different sizes to see which you prefer.

Trace the image onto tracing paper and then transfer it onto card. Simply cut around the traced outline of the card to produce your template. To get you started, a range of templates for some of the cookies created in this book can be found on p116–118.

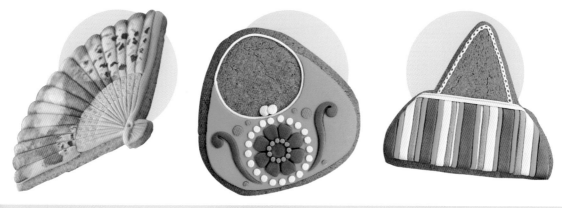

baking cookies

Fundamental to any decorated cookie is the taste and shape of the cookie itself. When choosing a recipe it's important to opt for one that retains its shape and doesn't spread too much whilst baking. The flavour and texture should also compliment the type of icing you plan to use. All the designs in this book can be made with any of the three basic dough recipes provided. Simply follow my tips on mixing, baking and storing to create fresh, crisp and tasty cookies every time.

mix it up

- ✿ Always use only the finest and freshest ingredients.

- ✿ Use unsalted butter. Try not to use substitute fats, spreadable butters and low calorie spreads. These can often ruin a recipe as they have added air and water in them and so change the consistency of the dough. Butter gives cookies their flavour and crisp outside texture.

- ✿ Make sure you carefully measure your ingredients. Baking requires accuracy.

- ✿ Mix the dry ingredients thoroughly before mixing in the liquids.

- ✿ Do not over-mix the dough as this will toughen it, just mix until the flour is incorporated.

- ✿ Most cookie dough can be prepared well in advance. Simply wrap the dough in cling film/plastic wrap and store it in a refrigerator or freezer.

baked to perfection

❀ Always preheat your oven.

❀ Make sure you leave room between cookies on the baking sheet to allow them to expand a little.

❀ Try to bake cookies of a similar size in the same batch to avoid over-baking smaller cookies.

❀ Place uncooked cookies on cool baking sheets. Rotate baking sheets and rinse and wipe clean between batches.

❀ Watch the baking time. Always check cookies at the minimum baking time – even one minute can mean the difference between a cookie that is done and one that is ruined.

❀ Cool cookies on wire racks. This will allow the steam to evaporate and will prevent your cookies from becoming soggy.

store them away

❀ Make the cookies up to one month in advance and store them un-iced in an airtight container in the freezer.

❀ Most cookies have a two week shelf life, so don't be afraid to start your baking well in advance.

I've provided three recipes for creating three delicious types of cookies, which are sure to be adored by all! Match the flavouring with the theme of your decoration, for example the Fruit Cocktails (p68) would be great in spiced orange and use gingerbread for the Home Sweet Home cookies (p48) for a rustic, comforting taste.

vanilla cookies

1 Preheat the oven to 170°C/325°F/ Gas Mark 3.

2 Place the dry ingredients in a mixing bowl. Add the butter and rub together with your fingertips until the mixture resembles fine breadcrumbs. Make a hollow in the centre and pour in the beaten egg, golden syrup and vanilla extract. Mix together well, until you have a ball of dough.

ingredients...

- ❀ 275g (10oz) plain flour, sifted
- ❀ 5ml (1 tsp) baking powder
- ❀ 100g (3½ oz) caster sugar
- ❀ 75g (3oz) butter, diced
- ❀ 1 small egg, beaten
- ❀ 30ml (2 tbsp) golden syrup
- ❀ 2.5ml (½ tsp) vanilla extract

3 Place the dough in a plastic bag and chill in the fridge for 30 minutes.
4 Roll the dough out on a lightly floured surface to 5mm (⅕in) thick and stamp out the cookies, using your chosen cutters. If you are using a template, cut around the template with a knife for each cookie.

If you are short of time you can buy plain cookies from the supermarket, ready to be decorated

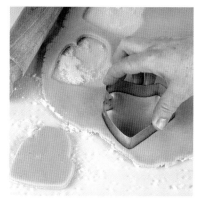

5 Lightly knead and re-roll the trimmings together again to use up all the dough. Place the cookies on greased baking sheets.

6 Bake for 12–15 minutes until lightly coloured and firm but not crisp. Leave on the tray for two minutes before transferring to a wire rack to cool completely.

spiced orange cookies

1 Preheat the oven to 170°C/325°F/ Gas Mark 3.

2 Place the butter, sugar, honey, orange zest and orange juice in a saucepan and heat gently until the sugar has dissolved and the butter melted.

3 Sieve the flour and dry ingredients in a bowl and add the melted ingredients. Mix well until the dough becomes firm.

4 Place the dough in a plastic bag and chill in the fridge for 40 minutes.

5 Continue as for the vanilla cookies. Bake for 10–15 minutes, depending on the size of your cookies.

ingredients...

- 🌸 75g (3oz) butter
- 🌸 75g (3oz) soft brown sugar
- 🌸 30ml (2 tbsp) honey
- 🌸 zest from one orange
- 🌸 10ml (2 tsp) orange juice
- 🌸 225g (8oz) plain flour, sifted
- 🌸 5ml (1 tsp) bicarbonate of soda
- 🌸 5ml (1 tsp) cinnamon

why not try adding the zest and juice of a lemon for zingy lemon-flavoured cookies?

gingerbread

For gingerbread men, try adding currants for eyes before baking

1 Preheat the oven to 170°C/ 325°F/ Gas Mark 3.

2 Place the butter, treacle and sugar into a saucepan and heat gently until the sugar has dissolved and the butter melted. Cool slightly.

3 Sieve the dry ingredients into a mixing bowl. Pour the melted mixture into the dry ingredients and stir.

4 Dissolve the bicarbonate of soda in the milk and add to the mixture. Combine to make a dough, adding more milk if necessary.

5 Place the dough in a plastic bag and chill in the fridge for 40 minutes.

6 Continue as for vanilla cookies then bake for 10–15 minutes, depending on the size of your cookies.

ingredients...

- 125g (4oz) butter
- 60ml (4 tbsp) black treacle
- 225g (8oz) soft brown sugar
- 450g (1 lb) plain flour
- 15ml (1 tbsp) ground ginger
- 7.5ml (1½ tsp) cinnamon
- 5ml (1 tsp) bicarbonate of soda
- 15ml (1 tbsp) milk

covering cookies

There are a number of edible materials that you can use to cover your cookies, from the classic royal icing to the more contemporary sugarpaste.

sugarpaste (rolled fondant)

This is a sweet, thick, opaque paste that is soft, pliable, easily coloured and extremely versatile. It is simple and inexpensive to make, just follow the recipe below to create 1kg (2¼lb). I used sugarpaste to decorate a range of cookies featured in this book as it is easy to shape and emboss to create stunning effects, such as the Dressed Up cookies on p70.

Ready-made sugarpaste is widely available and comes in a spectrum of colours

ingredients...

- 60ml (4 tbsp) cold water
- 20ml (4 tsp/1 sachet) powdered gelatine
- 125ml (4floz) liquid glucose
- 15ml (1 tbsp) glycerine
- 1kg (2¼lb) icing (confectioners') sieved sugar, plus extra for dusting

1 Place the water in a small bowl, sprinkle over the gelatine and soak until spongy. Stand the bowl over a pan of hot (not boiling) water and stir until the gelatine is dissolved. Add the glucose and glycerine, stirring until well blended and runny.

2 Put the icing sugar in a large bowl. Make a well in the centre and slowly pour in the liquid ingredients, stirring constantly. Mix well.

3 Turn out on to a surface dusted with icing sugar and knead until smooth, sprinkling with extra icing sugar if the paste becomes too sticky. The paste can be used immediately or tightly wrapped and stored until required.

Store sugarpaste in thick plastic bags in an airtight container

edible gums
Small quantities of these can be kneaded into sugarpaste to make it firmer and more versatile for decorating cookies and can be useful for details such as the bows and tassels of The Graduate (p44). The gum allows the sugarpaste to be rolled out more thinly and the soft paste to be modelled more easily. As a guide, add 5ml (1 tsp) gum to 225g (8oz) sugarpaste, less for firmer paste and more for sticky soft paste. You can use either of the following:

gum tragacanth is a natural gum that is excellent if you have time. Ideally, the gum needs time to work before the paste is used. You will begin to feel a difference in the paste after an hour or so, but it is best left overnight.

cmc is a synthetic substitute but has the advantage that it acts instantly. CMC is known by various names including Tylo Powder and Tylose.

royal icing

Royal icing has traditionally been the standard icing for covering cookies. Today, however, it is often just used to add fine piped detail to covered cookies, for example the Winged Beauty designs (p80). Royal icing is available in ready-to-mix packets but it is just as easy, and cheaper, to make your own.

Add 2.5ml (½ tsp) glycerine to the icing to prevent it setting too hard

ingredients...

- 🌼 1 egg white
- 🌼 250g (9oz) icing (confectioners') sugar, sifted

1 Beat the egg white in a bowl until foamy.

2 Gradually beat in the icing sugar until the icing is glossy and forms soft peaks.

3 If you are not using the icing immediately, cover it with plastic wrap to exclude the air until you are ready for it.

buttercream

Buttercream is used as a sweet covering which is soft, has a rich flavour and can be easily piped. I used it in the birthday cake for Baby's First Birthday (p58) to add an interesting texture.

Use white vegetable fat instead of butter to achieve a pure white 'buttercream'

1 Place the butter in a bowl and beat until light and fluffy. Sift the icing sugar into the bowl and continue to beat until the mixture changes colour.

2 Add just enough milk or water to give a firm but spreadable consistency.

3 Flavour by adding the vanilla or alternative flavouring. Store in an airtight container until required.

ingredients...

- ❀ 110g (3¾oz) unsalted (sweet) butter
- ❀ 350g (12oz) icing (confectioners') sugar
- ❀ 15–30ml (1–2 tbsp) milk or water
- ❀ a few drops of vanilla extract or alternative flavouring

piping gel

This is a multi-purpose transparent gel that is excellent for attaching sugarpaste to cookies, e.g. for the Happy Feet designs (p56). It can also add shimmering accents and colourful highlights to cookies. It is available commercially but is just as easy to make, using the recipe provided.

Once cooled, piping gel can be stored for up to two months

ingredients...

- ✤ 15ml (1 tbsp) powered gelatine
- ✤ 15ml (1 tbsp) cold water
- ✤ 250ml (9 fl oz /1 cup) light corn syrup (light Karo syrup) or liquid glucose

1 Sprinkle the gelatine over the cold water in a small saucepan and soak until spongy – about five minutes.

2 Heat on low until the gelatine has become clear and dissolved. Do not allow to boil.

3 Add syrup or glucose and heat thoroughly. Cool and store.

confectioners' glaze

This is available from cake decorating suppliers and can be used to add a glossy sheen. Mix it with edible lustre dust to create metallic edible paint, e.g. to the Crackers About You cookies (p108).

Be restrained when applying sugar glue. A little goes a long way

sugar glue

Although gum glues are commercially available, sugar glue is quick and substantially cheaper to make at home. It is used for attaching pieces of sugarpaste to each other, e.g. for the Funky Owl cookies (p88).

1 Break up pieces of sugarpaste into a small container and cover with a little boiling water.
2 Stir until dissolved. This produces a thick glue, which can be thinned easily by adding some more cooled boiled water.

white vegetable fat

This is a solid white vegetable fat (shortening), often known by a brand name: in the UK, Trex or White Flora; in South Africa, Holsum; in Australia, Copha and in America, Crisco. These products are more or less interchangeable. I use white vegetable fat as a lubricant to stop the paste sticking to the surface on to which it is being rolled out and to add shine, e.g. to the Hot Lips cookies (p76).

decorating cookies

Decorate your cookies using sugarpaste, royal icing, or a mixture of the two. Your choice will depend on the effects you wish to create and your taste preference.

using sugarpaste

Sugarpaste is an excellent and very versatile medium for cookie decorators as it allows the user to be extremely creative. Colour your paste by kneading in some edible food paste colour (not liquid as the paste will become too sticky) then follow the steps below to create a smooth surface covering for any cookie.

1 Smear white vegetable fat over your work surface to prevent the icing sticking. Knead the sugarpaste to warm it before use.

2 Roll out the kneaded sugarpaste to a thickness of 3mm (⅛in) and cut out a shape using the cookie cutter or template used to create the cookie. Remove the excess paste.

If the cookie cutter has left a ragged edge around the base of the shape, just carefully tuck this under with a finger before placing on the cookie

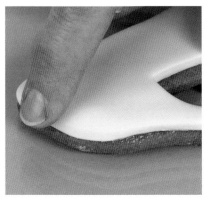

3 Paint piping gel over the top of the baked cookie to act as glue. Alternatively, use buttercream or boiled jam.

4 Carefully lift the sugarpaste shape using a palette knife, to prevent distorting the shape, and place on top of the cookie.

5 Run a finger around the top cut edge of the sugarpaste to smooth and curve.

using royal icing

Royal icing is a classic cookie icing that dries to form a smooth, hard layer. To create your icing, follow the recipe given on p20.

The icing should have soft peak consistency so adjust as necessary, adding either a little icing sugar or water as required

1 Divide the royal icing into small bowls and tint with edible colours.
2 Half fill a piping bag with icing then cut away a small section from the tip of the bag. Cover the remaining icing with plastic wrap to prevent a skin forming.

3 Pipe a steady smooth line around the outline of the cookie. Do this by touching the cookie with the tip of the bag and slowly squeezing out the icing by holding the icing bag above the cookie and letting the icing fall into place.

4 Dilute the remaining icing with a few drops of water to give a runny consistency and use to half fill another piping bag. Snip the end from the bag and flood the centre of the cookie, being careful not to let the icing overflow around the edges.

adding a pattern

1 While the royal icing is still wet, place some contrasting icing into a piping bag and pipe a pattern on to the wet icing.

2 If desired, use a cocktail stick to drag icing of one colour into another to create patterns. Leave to dry.

decorating tips

These tips and techniques will help you well on your way to using sugarpaste and royal icing to create professional-looking cookies that will truly impress. Always remember, it's only a cookie! Practise makes perfect and if the decoration doesn't quite work out as you'd planned, somebody will always be pleased to eat it.

piping dots

This technique is useful for adding iced bubbles, eyes and decorative beads to your creations.

1 The royal icing should have soft peak consistency so adjust as necessary by adding icing sugar or water as required. Aim to pipe dots, not pointed cones!
2 Use a reusable piping bag and coupler or a disposable piping bag, fitted with a suitable piping tube. Half fill the bag with royal icing.
3 Hold the tip of the tube just above your cookie and gently squeeze out icing to produce a dot. Gradually lift the tip of the tube as the dot increases in size. Once it is of an appropriate size, stop squeezing, hold for a second and then remove the piping tube.

If your dots are slightly pointed, use a damp paintbrush to quickly knock them back

using a sugar shaper

A sugar shaper is a very useful tool that comes with 16 different discs, allowing paste to be squeezed out in different shapes to make tassels, flower centres, sausages and more. The secret of success is to use paste of the correct consistency.

1 Knead in some gum to your sugarpaste (see p19) to give the paste stretch.
2 Knead in some white vegetable fat to stop the paste getting sticky. Partially dunk the paste into a small container of boiled water before kneading again (the paste should have the consistency of chewing gum).
3 Place the softened paste together with your chosen disc into the sugar shaper. Squeeze out a length of paste from the shaper, carefully remove it with a Dresden tool (see p9) and attach to your cookie.

cutting out flowers

I used sugarpaste flowers on several of my cookie designs to give them a fresh, feminine look. They are so quick and easy to create; use the following technique for intricate flower shapes.

1 Knead in some gum to your sugarpaste (see p19) then thinly roll out the paste.
2 To achieve a clean cut, rather than pressing the flower cutter into the paste as you would a simple flower, place the paste over the cutter and roll over with a rolling pin.
3 Run your finger over the edges of the cutter, turn it over and carefully press out the paste from the cutter, using a soft paintbrush.

cookie creations...

so in love...

white wedding

These oh-so-elegant cookies are as beautiful as the bride and will look simply divine as favours at your wedding.

you will need...

- 🌸 tiered wedding cake shaped cookies
- 🌸 sugarpaste: white or ivory
- 🌸 tiered wedding cake cutter
- 🌸 piping gel
- 🌸 flower cutter: flat floral collection set 1 (lc)
- 🌸 ball tool (fmm)
- 🌸 reusable piping bag and coupler
- 🌸 royal icing
- 🌸 piping tubes no. 1, 2 & 3 (pme)
- 🌸 edible snowflake lustre dust (sk)

Covering

1 Prepare the cookies as shown on p14–17.

2 Roll out the white or ivory sugarpaste to a thickness of 3mm (⅛in) and cut out the tiered cake shape using the cutter used to create the cookie. Attach in place on the cookies using piping gel.

Decorating

1 Emboss the tiers with the flower cutter and use the end of a ball tool to indent the centre of each petal.

2 Fill a piping bag fitted with a coupler with royal icing and attach a no. 1 piping tube. Pipe a row of dots at the base of each tier to help define the tiers.

3 Attach a no. 2 tube on to the piping bag and pipe loose coils, as shown in the picture opposite.

4 Attach a no. 3 tube and carefully pipe the centre of each flower. Using the same tube, pipe a small dot in the space between the petals.

5 To add shine, dust over the cookie with edible snowflake lustre dust.

For a sparkling finish, add the lustre dust before the sugarpaste dries

back to basics cookie recipes p14–17... sugarpaste p18... royal icing p20...

always the bridesmaid

These simply stylish shoes make the perfect wedding favour for a special bridesmaid. Coordinate the colour of the sugarpaste with your own wedding colour scheme.

you will need...

- high heel shoe shaped cookies
- sugarpaste: pale mint, light grey, dark brown
- high heel shoe cutter (lc)
- cutting wheel (pme)
- craft knife
- stitching wheel (pme)
- mini embosser (hp set 10)
- royal icing
- edible silver lustre dust (sk)

Covering

Prepare the cookies as shown on p14–17. Roll out the pale mint sugarpaste to a thickness of 3mm (⅛in). Cut out the shoe shape using the high heel shoe cutter used to create the cookie and place on top of the cookie.

Decorating

Mark the line between the heel and shoe with a cutting wheel. Using a craft knife, cut away the tip of the heel, the sole and a thin tapered strip from the top of the shoe for the lining. Run a stitching wheel around the upper edge of the shoe. Use the mini embosser to emboss a floral pattern on the shoe. For the lining, thinly roll out some light grey sugarpaste and, using the cookie cutter and a cutting wheel, cut a shape to fit. Attach and trim as necessary. Next, carefully replace the cut away sections of the heel and sole with dark brown sugarpaste.

Adding embellishment

Pipe flower centres using royal icing. Mix the edible silver lustre dust with boiled water or clear alcohol and paint over the lining to finish.

back to basics   cookie recipes p14–17... sugarpaste p18... royal icing p20...

wonky wonder

Decorate these funky, three-tiered cookie cakes in any way you desire to make a big impression at any wedding or party.

you will need...

- ❀ wonky wedding cake shaped cookies
- ❀ sugarpaste: selection of pink shades
- ❀ piping gel
- ❀ royal icing
- ❀ wonky wedding cake cutter (lc)
- ❀ palette knife
- ❀ gum tragacanth or cmc (optional)
- ❀ small flower cutters (pme)
- ❀ reusable piping bag and coupler
- ❀ selection of round piping tubes, e.g. no. 0, 1, 2, 3 (pme)

Covering

Prepare the cookies as shown on p14–17. Roll out the various pink sugarpastes to a thickness of 3mm (⅛in). To create the stripes, cut out thin strips of each shade and place vertically on to the bottom tier of the cookie, attaching them in place with piping gel. Trim to fit then add a base strip of dark pink paste in the same way. Use the cookie cutter to cut light and dark pink paste for the upper tiers and lift on to the cookie with a palette knife.

Decorating

Adding the flowers Thinly roll out the sugarpaste, adding gum if necessary for firmness. Use appropriate cutters to cut out a selection of small flowers and flower centres from various shades of pink sugarpaste and attach in place.

Adding the bubbles Fill a piping bag fitted with a coupler with royal icing and attach a piping tube. Pipe dots onto the top tier as desired, checking the consistency of your icing to avoid pointed peaks. Change the tube size and repeat.

back to basics   cookie recipes p14–17... sugarpaste p18... royal icing p20...

bride and groom

What better way to celebrate that special day than with this beautifully attired pair? Together they make up a unique gift that the happy couple will never forget!

you will need...

- heart-shaped cookies
- sugarpaste: ivory, cream, claret, black
- heart-shaped cutter
- mini embossers e.g. set 1, 2, 10 (hp)
- cutting wheel
- small flower cutters e.g. flower plunger cutters (pme)
- royal icing
- edible snowflake dust (sk)
- Groom template p116
- dresden tool
- edible gold dust (sk)

For the bride

1 Prepare the heart-shaped cookie. Roll out white or ivory sugarpaste to a thickness of 3mm (⅛in). Cut a heart shape, then use a cutting wheel to cut away the top section. Carefully lift on to the cookie.

2 Use the mini embossers to decorate the top of the dress with leaves and flowers. Run a cutting wheel over the the lower section of the heart for a textured ribbon effect.

3 Use the small cutters to cut out three flowers, placing the smaller ones inside the largest, and attach in place. Carefully pipe royal icing dots to create a necklace. Dust the icing with snowflake dust to add sparkle.

For the groom

1 Prepare the heart-shaped cookie. Using the template on p116, cut sugarpaste and attach as follows: the white shirt, the claret tie (adding texture with a Dresden tool), the white collar, the cream waistcoat, the black jacket body and, finally, the lapels.

2 Model buttons from small balls of cream sugarpaste and attach to the waistcoat. Create a buttonhole by pinching the petals of plunger flowers together and attach.

3 Mix the edible gold dust together with a little boiled water and use a fine paintbrush to apply delicate detail to the waistcoat.

back to basics   cookie recipes p14–17... sugarpaste p18... royal icing p20...

heartfelt centrepiece

Make a statement with this stunning arrangement of intricately decorated hearts. The addition of individual packaging adds a truly professional touch.

you will need...

- heart-shaped cookies in various sizes and flavours
- sugarpaste: white or ivory
- set of heart-shaped cookie cutters e.g. nesting heart set (w)
- piping gel
- palette knife
- selection of embossers
- royal icing
- edible snowflake lustre dust (sk)
- white hologram disco dust (ea)

To create the embellished hearts

1 Prepare a variety of heart cookies as shown on p14–17. Roll out white or ivory sugarpaste to a thickness of 3mm (⅛in) and cut out the heart shapes using different sized cutters. Paint piping gel over the top of each cookie to act as glue. Carefully lift sugarpaste hearts into place on each cookie using a palette knife.

2 Experiment with a selection of embossers as desired. You could try using stick embossers, floral stamps, textured rolling pins and flower and heart cutters. Add piped royal iced dots as desired.

3 Add sparkle by dusting each covered cookie with snowflake lustre dust before the sugarpaste dries. Then add a light covering of white hologram disco dust to finish.

To create the centrepiece

Place each cookie in a clear cookie bag and tie up with ribbon. Hang the bagged cookies on a display tree and place in the centre of your table.

You can use the same design for each cookie, or embellish each one individually

back to basics   cookie recipes p14–17... sugarpaste p18... royal icing p20...

musical inspirations

If music be the food of love, these striking musical notes are sure to be adored by all! A special occasion always demands music, so these 'musical cookies' are the perfect accompaniment to any event.

They are so simple to create: Decorate the notes with coloured royal icing (see pages 20 and 26–27). You can have lots of fun jazzing them up with a variety of zingy colours and bold patterns, such as the hearts, flowers and swirls I have used here. To make the music, cover cookies with sugarpaste, mark the staves with a cutting wheel and cut treble clefs and notes from paste using music cutters (FMM).

Be as subtle or bright as you like; try classical cream and black, or funky fuchsia and lime green.

43

the graduate

Whatever they are graduating from, show just how proud you are of their achievements with these first class mortarboard and scroll cookies.

you will need...

- ❀ mortarboard and scroll-shaped cookies
- ❀ sugarpaste: black, parchment, red
- ❀ mortar board and certificate cutters (cg)
- ❀ cutting wheel
- ❀ gum tragacanth/ cmc/tylose
- ❀ sugar shaper

Cut dovetails in the end of the ribbon for a sophisticated look

Covering

For the mortarboard Prepare the cookies as shown on p14–17 and cover with black sugarpaste. Use a cutting wheel to mark two lines to define the lower half of the mortar board, then run the cutting wheel 5mm (⅕in) from the lower edge to create a rim to the cap.

For the scroll Prepare the cookies and cover with parchment-coloured sugarpaste. Use a cutting wheel to create a curved line to define the end section, then add concentric circles on to the end of the scroll.

Decorating

Making the tassel Soften some red sugarpaste (see p19). Place the paste together with a mesh disc into the sugar shaper and gently squeeze out a 9cm (3½in) tassel. Attach in place and top with a red ball.

Creating the bow Thinly roll out the red paste and cut into 2cm (⅘in) wide strips. Place one strip around the centre of the certificate. Create a bow with the remaining strips. Finish by wrapping a 1cm (⅜in) wide band around the centre of the bow.

back to basics cookie recipes p14–17... sugarpaste p18...

shop 'til you drop

Spoil your mum on Mother's Day by appealing to her shopaholic side. The instructions below are for my pretty floral bag but these cookies can be embellished to represent her favourite store.

you will need...

- 🌼 shopping bag shaped cookies
- 🌼 sugarpaste: deep cream, blue, brown, dark brown, green
- 🌼 shopping bag cookie cutters (lc)
- 🌼 cutting wheel
- 🌼 gum tragacanth/cmc/tylose (optional)
- 🌼 daisy cutter: daisy chain (pc)
- 🌼 craft knife
- 🌼 edible gold lustre dust (sk)
- 🌼 sugar shaper (optional)

Covering

Prepare the cookies as shown on p14–17 and cover with blue sugarpaste. Cut a vertical line from the lowest bottom corner up to the top of the bag and remove the small end section. Replace this section with deep cream sugarpaste and mark a crease with a cutting wheel.

Decorating

Adding embellishments Thinly roll out some cream and green sugarpaste, adding gum if necessary for firmness. Use the daisy cutter to emboss the daisy and leaves on to the paste, then take a craft knife and cut around the required pieces. Arrange on the cookie as desired. Mix some lustre dust with boiled water and paint on your own designer name.

Attaching the handles Fit a sugar shaper with a small round disc and squeeze out two short lengths of dark cream paste. Alternatively, thinly roll two small sausages of paste with your fingers. Attach to the top of the bag as shown.

back to basics cookie recipes p14–17... sugarpaste p18...

home sweet home

These cookies are so simple to make and will make a great welcome home gift. For a personal touch, the shape of the cookie can be easily tailored to suit the recipient's own home.

you will need...

- ❀ template p117 or image of the new home
- ❀ stiff card
- ❀ barbeque skewers
- ❀ cocktail sticks
- ❀ 2mm aluminium wire
- ❀ wire cutters
- ❀ non toxic glue
- ❀ cookie dough
- ❀ icing sugar

Resize your home image on a computer or photocopier

Preparing the dough

1 Transfer a template or your own line drawing of a house onto the stiff card. Cut barbeque skewers and cocktail sticks to fit the lines and details of the template and use aluminium wire to fit any curved elements. Attach these with non toxic glue and allow the glue to dry.

2 Roll out the cookie dough so that it is 3mm (⅛in) thicker than the house embosser. Place your card house on top, card side upper most, and roll over it firmly with a rolling pin to transfer the details on to the dough.

3 Gently peel back the template and use a knife to carefully cut around the outside of the cookie. Touch up any detail as necessary. Transfer to a baking sheet and bake (see p12–13).

Decorating

Once the cookies have cooled, liberally sprinkle icing sugar over them to fill the indented lines. Carefully brush away the excess sugar with a small brush to reveal the detail on the cookies.

back to basics cookie recipes p14–17... templates p11...

trick or treat

These spooky cookies are sure to go down a treat with the children at Halloween and they will love to get involved with making them, too. Simply prepare the cookies as on p14–17 and let them loose with the decoration.

you will need...

- ❀ halloween cookies: cat, moon, pumpkin, witch's hat, ghost, bat
- ❀ sugarpaste: black, white, orange, cream
- ❀ halloween cookie cutters: cat, moon, pumpkin, witch's hat, ghost, bat
- ❀ dresden tool
- ❀ cutting wheel
- ❀ piping tubes: no. 4, no.18 (pme)
- ❀ ball tool (fmm)

Witch's hat Cover with black sugarpaste and add folds by pressing a Dresden tool into the soft paste.

Moon Cover with cream sugarpaste and indent the smile with a cutting wheel. Remove the eye with a no. 18 tube and replace with a ball of white paste. Add a smaller ball for the pupil and finish off with white paste for a light spot. Mould a small sausage of paste for the eyebrow and attach. Add texture by indenting the surface of the moon with a ball tool.

Pumpkin Cover with orange sugarpaste and create ridges in the surface by pulling the wider end of a Dresden tool through the soft paste. Add a stalk and texture with the sharp end of a Dresden tool.

Ghost Cover with white paste and add movement by stroking the soft paste to give slight indentations. Add a smile and eyes by using both ends of the no. 4 piping tube to cut shapes from black sugarpaste.

Bat and cat Cover with black sugarpaste and texture using the cutting wheel and Dresden tool. Add small balls of paste for eyes.

back to basics cookie recipes p14–17... sugarpaste p18...

up, up and away

This oh-so-colourful collection of fun balloons will brighten up any birthday party. Children will love picking their favourite colour and eating the cookies like lollipops.

you will need...

- ❀ balloon-shaped cookies
- ❀ cookie sticks
- ❀ sugarpaste: lime green, pink, light blue, yellow, white
- ❀ balloon cookie cutters
- ❀ piping gel
- ❀ cutting wheel
- ❀ gum tragacanth/ cmc/tylose (optional)

Ensure your cookies are thick enough to insert the sticks without them showing

Preparing

Prepare the cookies as shown on p14–17, bake and insert a cookie stick into each cookie just as they come out of the oven, before they cool and harden.

Covering

Cover each cookie with your colour choice of sugarpaste, using piping gel as glue. Use a cutting wheel to mark a line between the balloon and its tied end and an additional line at the end of the tie.

Decorating

Thinly roll out some white sugarpaste, adding gum if necessary for firmness. Use the cutting wheel to cut a 7mm x 3cm (¼ x 1⅕in) wide strip for each cookie. Curve each strip and attach to the balloons to represent light spots.

Making the centrepiece

Fill a suitable container full of sweets and arrange the cookies as desired. You may wish to cut the sticks of some shorter in order to achieve a pleasing arrangement. Alternatively, place the sticks into some florist's Staysoft, Oasis or polystyrene and cover with coloured tissue paper or sisal.

back to basics   cookie recipes p14–17... sugarpaste p18... piping gel p22...

springtime joy

Bring the joys of spring into your kitchen with this playful parade of colourful cookies. Experiment with a range of cookie cutters to create leaping lambs, bouncing bunnies, cute chicks and delightful tulips. Use a cutting wheel (pme) to mark the rabbit's ears and tulip petals and define the shape of the rabbit using the Dresden tool (fmm).

You can also find a wide range of embossers to embellish the cookies. They certainly make a refreshing alternative to traditional chocolate Easter eggs!

Use a sugar shaper fitted with a mesh disc to create realistically textured details for the wool, tails and feathers.

hey baby

happy feet

These adorable footprint cookies are simple to make and perfect for celebrating the birth of twins. Use royal icing to add the babies' names for a personal touch.

you will need...

- ❀ foot-shaped cookies
- ❀ sugarpaste: pastel blue or pink
- ❀ template p117
- ❀ cutting wheel
- ❀ piping gel or boiled jam
- ❀ small oval cutters (lc)
- ❀ piping bag
- ❀ royal icing, coloured as appropriate

Covering

1 Prepare the cookies as shown on p14–17. Roll out the pink or blue sugarpaste to a thickness of 3mm (⅛in) and, with a cutting wheel or knife, cut out the instep using the template on p117.

2 Lightly spread piping gel or boiled jam over the top of the baked cookie to act as glue. Carefully lift the sugarpaste using a palette knife to prevent the shape distorting and place in position on top of the cookie. Run a finger around the cut edge of the sugarpaste to smooth and curve.

3 For toes, cut ovals of a suitable size from sugarpaste and attach in the same way.

Decorating

Fill a piping bag with dark pink or blue royal icing and carefully pipe the desired names directly on to the instep of the cookies.

Personalize the cookies with the time and date of birth and baby's weight

back to basics cookie recipes p14–17... sugarpaste p18... royal icing p20...

baby's first birthday

Mark your little one's landmark occasion with these scrummy cookies. I used chocolate sweets to decorate them but you can replace these with your child's favourite treat.

you will need...

- ❀ number one and cupcake-shaped cookies
- ❀ sugarpaste: red, orange
- ❀ number one and cupcake cookie cutters (lc)
- ❀ piping gel
- ❀ sweets of your choice
- ❀ palette knife
- ❀ piping bag and large star tube
- ❀ buttercream

Decorating

Prepare the cookies as shown on p14–17.

For the number one Roll out sugarpaste to a thickness of 3mm (⅛in) and cut out ones, using the cookie cutter used to create the cookie. Place the sugarpaste on top of the cookies and attach sweets using piping gel to ensure they stick.

For the cupcake Paint piping gel over the lower half of the cookie. Roll out the red sugarpaste and cut out a cupcake using the cupcake cutter. Cut away the top of the sugarpaste to leave just the cupcake case shape and carefully place on the cookie. Use a palette knife to emboss vertical lines on to the cupcake case to represent the folds. Place a star tube on to a piping bag, fill with soft buttercream and pipe swirls over the top of the cookie. To decorate, push sweets into the swirls as desired.

back to basics cookie recipes p14–17... sugarpaste p18... buttercream p21...

sweet smiles

These cute cookies are sure to make you smile! Use bright, bold colours for a birthday party, or choose soft pastel tones and give the cookies as a special gift for a christening.

you will need...

- ❀ round cookies
- ❀ piping gel
- ❀ sugarpaste: pastel shades
- ❀ round cookie or pastry cutters
- ❀ reusable piping bag and coupler
- ❀ piping tubes: no. 1, 2, 3 (pme)
- ❀ royal icing

For the best results, ensure your royal icing is the correct consistency

Covering

1 Prepare the cookies as shown on p14–17. Paint piping gel over the cookies to act as glue.

2 Roll out pastel sugarpaste to a thickness of 3mm (⅛in) and cut out the circle shapes using round cookie or pastry cutters. Carefully place on to each cookie. Run a finger around the cut edge of the sugarpaste to smooth and curve the edges.

Decorating

1 Take a circle cutter of a suitable size and emboss it centrally into the soft paste for the face, e.g. for 6cm (2⅓in) cookies use a 3.5cm (1⅓in) circle cutter.

2 Fill a piping bag with royal icing and fit the no. 3 tube to the coupler. Pipe a circle of icing over the embossed circle.

3 To give a softer appearance to the face, use a damp paintbrush to gently stroke the inner edge of the piped circle towards the centre of the cookie.

4 Change the tube to no. 2 and carefully pipe the facial expression, referring to the photo opposite for ideas. For finer details, change to a no. 1 tube.

back to basics cookie recipes p14–17... sugarpaste p18... royal icing p20...

baby shower bootees

Babies' bootees are just so gorgeous and their shape makes them perfect for creating these sweet little cookies for a baby shower. The instructions here are for the striped sock but the picture opposite gives you further decorative ideas.

you will need...

- ❀ sock-shaped cookies
- ❀ piping gel
- ❀ sugarpaste: pale pink, pink, deep pink, pale green, green, orange
- ❀ sock cookie cutter (lc)
- ❀ template p116
- ❀ card
- ❀ cutting wheel
- ❀ sugar glue
- ❀ craft knife
- ❀ sugar shaper

Covering

Prepare the cookies as shown on p14–17. Paint piping gel over each cookie and cover with sugarpaste. Cut out with the sock cookie cutter.

Decorating

Adding the heel, toe and cuff Trace the template at the back of the book and transfer to card. Cut out the heel, toe and top sections. Thinly roll out your chosen colours. Place the card sections on to the rolled out paste and cut around each with a cutting wheel. Attach the sections to the cookie using sugar glue.

Adding stripes Thinly roll out two colours of paste and cut 7mm (¼in) strips of paste from one colour and 3mm (⅛in) strips of paste from another. Paint lines of sugar glue on to the cookie and place the strips on top. Trim off the excess with a craft knife. Soften one of the pastes and place in a sugar shaper together with a small, round disc (see p29). Squeeze out a length of paste and add to the stripe pattern. Repeat.

back to basics cookie recipes p14–17... sugarpaste p18... sugar glue p23...

just for mum

Make a new mum feel special with prettily embellished heart-shaped cookies; a collection of mini hearts in coordinating colours completes the set.

you will need...

- 🌸 large and small heart cookies
- 🌸 sugarpaste: lilac, pale pink, pink, silver
- 🌸 nesting heart cutter set (w)
- 🌸 piping gel
- 🌸 flower plunger cutters (pme)
- 🌸 sugar glue
- 🌸 edible silver lustre dust

A batch of mini hearts is a quick but stunning gift for any occasion

To create the embellished heart

1 Prepare the cookies as shown on p14–17. Roll out the pale pink sugarpaste to a thickness of 3mm (⅛in) and cut out a heart using the cookie cutter used to create the cookie.

2 Paint piping gel over the top of the baked cookie to act as glue, then carefully place the sugarpaste on top of the cookie.

3 Thinly roll out the remaining colours of sugarpaste and cut hearts in different sizes. Layer centrally on top of the covered cookie, using sugar glue or water to secure.

4 Cut a selection of small flowers using the plunger cutters and attach to the cookie as shown. Press the end of a paintbrush into the centre of each flower to add more interest.

5 As a finishing touch, mix silver lustre dust with boiled water and stipple over the silver sugarpaste.

To create the small hearts

Cover the small cookies with sugarpaste in a selection of coordinating colours, smoothing and curving the edges as for the large cookie.

back to basics cookie recipes p14–17... sugarpaste p18... piping gel p22...

hey boy, hey girl!

To make cookie gifts that any small child will adore, look out for nursery-themed cutters, such as teddies and toys. Simply adapting colours can make them suitable for a boy or girl. To add texture to the rocking horse, I used a sugar shaper fitted with a mesh disc for the mane and the tail. I also made the purple ball quite tactile by piping royal icing dots on to the purple round. Experimenting with sugarcraft techniques can be so much fun, it's child's play!

For realistic teddy fur, use the pointed end of a Dresden tool to repeatedly flick up small sections of paste.

girls, girls, girls

fruit cocktails

Just what you need for a fun night out with the girls! I've given instructions for the zingy green cocktail here, but experiment with coloured sugarpaste to create your favourite tipple.

you will need...

- 🎀 cocktail glass-shaped cookies
- 🎀 sugarpaste: white, red, deep green, green, pale yellow
- 🎀 cocktail glass cookie cutters (lc)
- 🎀 cutting wheel
- 🎀 dresden tool
- 🎀 paste colours: green, yellow

For the cocktail glass

1 Prepare the cookies as shown on p14–17.

2 Roll out white sugarpaste to a thickness of 3mm (⅛in) and cut out a glass shape. With a cutting wheel, make a 'V' cut at the base of the bowl of the glass and remove the top of the glass, leaving just the stem. Place the stem on the cookie.

3 Roll out green and cream sugarpaste to a thickness of 3mm (⅛in) and use the cutting wheel to cut into 2.5cm (1in) wide strips. Place them adjacent to each other and, with a finger, stroke one colour over another to give a partially mixed appearance. Flatten the paste with a rolling pin. Using the cookie cutter and cutting wheel, cut out the striped paste to form the bowl of the glass and position on the cookie.

For the pineapple

1 Thickly roll out the yellow paste, cut out a triangle and add texture by pressing a Dresden tool deeply into the soft paste. Using the cookie cutter, cut the shape to fit the glass and attach to the cookie. Add a cherry, rolled from red paste.

2 Mix the green and yellow paste colours separately with cooled boiled water. Paint green horizontal lines over the green section of the glass and yellow over the pineapple.

---

back to basics cookie recipes p14–17... sugarpaste p18...

dressed up

No girl will be able to resist these fabulous dresses! Find your inner designer and experiment with decoration to create cookies that are always in fashion.

you will need...

- 🎀 dress-shaped cookies
- 🎀 sugarpaste: red, black
- 🎀 dress cookie cutter (cg)
- 🎀 cutting wheel
- 🎀 mini flower embosser (hp set 1)
- 🎀 gum tragacanth/cmc/ tylose
- 🎀 indian scrolls cutter (lc)

Cover sugarpaste with plastic before using to prevent it drying out

Covering

Prepare the cookies as shown on p14–17. Roll a small, marble-sized ball of sugarpaste for each cookie, cut in half and attach the to the chest area of the cookie. Roll out red and black sugarpaste to a thickness of 3mm (⅛in) and cut out each dress, using the cookie cutter used to create the cookies.

Decorating

For the red dress Use a cutting wheel to stroke through the sugarpaste to create the textured skirt. Repeatedly pull the wheel down towards and through the hemline to create a feathered effect. Position the dress on the cookie and stroke the paste to fit the bust area. Finish by embossing the soft paste with the flower embosser around the top of the skirt, the top of the dress and between the bust.

For the black and red dress For the red decoration, add a little gum to the red sugarpaste (see p19) and thinly roll out. Use the Indian scrolls cutter to cut out scrolls and a cutting wheel to cut a few thin strips. Add a band of red paste under the bust line, then decorate the dress with the red strips and scrolls, curving the shapes to create an interesting pattern.

back to basics cookie recipes p14–17... sugarpaste p18...

tea with the girls

Inspired by art deco style and the ceramic paintings of Clarice Cliff, this teapot and matching cups are just the right combination of vintage style and funky finish.

you will need...

- retro teapot and cup cookies
- sugarpaste: cream, black, orange
- retro tea cookie cutter set (lc)
- piping gel
- cup and pot templates (p118)
- tracing paper
- small sharp scissors
- craft knife
- scriber
- cutting wheel
- sugar glue
- paste colours: red, orange, black

Covering

1 Roll out the cream sugarpaste to a thickness of 3mm (⅛in) and cut out a pot and cups. Cover the cookies with piping gel and place the sugarpaste pieces on top.

2 Trace the cup and pot templates on p118 on to tracing paper. Cut out the hole between the handle and the cup/pot with sharp scissors. Place the pot template over the pot cookie and cut around this hole with a craft knife. Remove the paste to reveal the cookie below. Repeat for the cups.

3 Scribe the lines from the pot template on to the pot cookie using a scriber tool or pin. Remove the template and run a cutting wheel over these scribed lines to help define the shape of the pot. Repeat for the cups.

Decorating

1 Thinly roll out the orange paste. Using the template and cutting wheel, cut out pot and cup handles; attach with sugar glue. Cut thin strips of both black and orange paste to decorate the edges of each cup and the pot as shown.

2 Dilute the paste colours separately in clear spirit or boiled water, then paint the blocks of colour on to the cookies. Ensure that all your brush strokes go in the same direction on each block of colour.

back to basics cookie recipes p14–17... sugarpaste p18... sugar glue p23...

bag it up

Eye-catching evening bags are a girl's best friend. Get creative with a range of cutters and trendy sugarpaste colours to create cookies with bags of style.

you will need...

- evening bag shaped cookies
- piping gel
- sugarpaste: turquoise, dark jade, pink, gold
- evening bag cookie cutter (lc)
- cutting wheel
- gum tragacanth /cmc/tylose
- white vegetable fat
- sugar shaper
- flower cutter (lc: flat floral)
- indian scrolls cutter (lc)

Covering

For the evening bag Prepare the cookies as shown on p14–17. Paint piping gel over the lower half of each cookie. Roll out sugarpaste to a thickness of 3mm (⅛in) and cut out the evening bag shape using the cutter used to create the cookie. Carefully lift in place on to each cookie. Using a cutting wheel or circle cutter, cut away the circular handle area to leave a bag shape.

For the handle Knead a little gum into the gold sugarpaste then add white vegetable fat and a little boiled water to soften. Place the paste together with the small round disc into the sugar shaper and gently squeeze out a length. Paint a piping gel handle on to the cookie then place the gold length on top and cut to size.

Decorating

Add a little gum to the coloured sugarpaste (see p19). Thinly roll out the paste and cut out your choice of flowers, scrolls, stripes or circles and arrange as desired. Use the photos opposite and on page 11 for inspiration.

back to basics cookie recipes p14–17... sugarpaste p18... piping gel p22...

hot lips

Make sure your loved one is thinking of you this Valentine's Day by sending him the sweetest kiss. These juicy lips are simply irresistible!

you will need...

- ❀ lip-shaped cookies
- ❀ white vegetable fat
- ❀ piping gel
- ❀ lip cutter
- ❀ card
- ❀ sugarpaste: red and black
- ❀ cutting wheel
- ❀ paintbrush

1 Prepare the cookies as shown on p14–17.

2 Smear white vegetable fat over your work surface to prevent the icing sticking.

3 Paint piping gel over the top of a baked cookie to act as glue.

4 Make a template for the lips using your cookie cutter (see p11). Add the shaped line separating the two lips to the template.

5 Roll a 2cm (⅘in) wide sausage of red sugarpaste and cut in half. Place one sausage of red sugarpaste over one lip on the template and mould to shape by stroking the soft paste with your fingers – refer to the picture opposite for guidance. Cut away the excess paste with a cutting wheel. Attach the lip to the cookie and repeat the process for the second lip.

6 For a shiny lip gloss effect, dip a paintbrush into white vegetable fat and paint over the lips with deliberate strokes.

Use a shade of pink or red sugarpaste to match your favourite lipstick

back to basics cookie recipes p14–17... sugarpaste p18... piping gel p22...

life's a beach

Bring back those happy holiday memories with this cute collection of beach-inspired cookies. You can find a wide selection of themed cutters, such as these flip flops (lc), bathing suits (cg) and ice cream cones (w) and it's easy to add a feminine twist by using smaller flower cutters for embellishment. Pastel sugarpaste colours are great for evoking those girly days out on the beach – try roughly mixing together two different coloured pastes for an interesting marbled effect. These are so quick and easy to create; you'll soon be escaping to the sunshine!

For truly tempting ice-cream, use marbled paste and flick up small sections to give a rough appearance.

designer style

winged beauties

These butterfly cookies are simply stunning and would make a great birthday gift. Make each cookie uniquely beautiful by piping a design of your choice.

you will need...

- butterfly-shaped cookies
- sugarpaste: pastel pink, orange, blue, white
- butterfly cookie cutters
- piping gel or boiled jam
- selection of small sugarcraft cutters
- piping bag & coupler
- piping tube no. 1, 2 (pme)
- royal icing

Covering

Prepare the cookies as shown on p14–17.

For the wings Roll out your choice of sugarpaste to 3mm (⅛in) and cut out a butterfly, using the cookie cutter used to create the cookies. Paint piping gel or boiled jam around the edge of the butterfly cookie and place the sugarpaste on top.

For the body Model a tapered cone from white sugarpaste and attach. Roll white sugarpaste into a ball and attach for the head.

Decorating

1 Take a small sugarcraft cutter and carefully press it into the soft paste all the way through to the cookie. Remove and repeat on the other wing of the butterfly. Repeat using other cutters until you have a symmetrical design. Remove the sugarpaste from within each shape.

2 Fill a piping bag fitted with a coupler and no. 1 tube with royal icing and carefully pipe dots as desired. Change the size of the tube and pipe larger dots.

back to basics cookie recipes p14–17... sugarpaste p18... royal icing p20...

patchwork pieces

These bright and colourful square designs were inspired by patchwork as the combination of patterns and colours look stunning when placed together.

you will need...

- ❀ square cookies
- ❀ sugarpaste: purple, red, pink, bronze
- ❀ square cutter
- ❀ piping gel
- ❀ mini embossers (hp)
- ❀ craft knife
- ❀ cutters: flower (lc: flat floral set 1), scalloped diamond (lc)
- ❀ edible bronze lustre dust (sk)
- ❀ daisy centre stamps (jem)
- ❀ piping tube no. 4 (pme)

Covering

1 Prepare the cookies as shown on p14–17. Roll out the pink sugarpaste to 3mm (⅛in), cut a square to fit the cookie and attach with piping gel.

2 Thinly roll out the purple paste, adding gum if needed (see p19) and emboss as desired. Cut a strip from the embossed paste and attach across one corner of the cookie. Cut cleanly to size using a craft knife.

Decorating

1 Roll thin sausages of bronze paste (using a sugar shaper if you have one), attach to either side of the purple strip and trim.

2 Cut a red strip from thinly rolled red paste, attach diagonally across the cookie and trim.

3 Thinly roll out the bronze paste and use the cutters to cut out flowers. Remove a circle from the centre of each petal using the piping tube. Attach to the cookie and cut to fit with the craft knife.

4 Mix the bronze lustre dust with the confectioners' glaze or boiled water and paint over the bronze areas of the cookie with a small brush to give a metallic effect.

5 Finally, create flower centres using the daisy stamps and purple paste and attach.

back to basics   cookie recipes p14–17... sugarpaste p18... confectioners' glaze p22...

indian elephants

These wonderfully decorated elephants are so eye-catching and make a great gift. Wrap them individually, adding decorations to compliment the cookies.

you will need...

- 🌸 elephant-shaped cookies
- 🌸 sugarpaste: brown/grey, red, pink, burgundy, dark green, gold
- 🌸 elephant-shaped cookie cutters
- 🌸 dresden tool
- 🌸 template (p116)
- 🌸 cutting wheel
- 🌸 mini embossers (hp)
- 🌸 piping bag and no. 1 tube (pme)
- 🌸 edible gold lustre dust (sk)
- 🌸 royal icing

Covering

Prepare the cookies as shown on p14–17. Roll out the brown/grey sugarpaste to 3mm (⅛in) and cut out elephants, using the cookie cutter used to create the cookies. Attach in place and use the Dresden tool to indent the eyes and mouths.

Decorating

1 Using the template on p116 and a cutting wheel, cut out the decoration for the elephants from thinly rolled paste, adding a little gum if necessary (see p19). Texture the sugarpaste as desired using mini embossers and piping tubes and attach in place.

2 Cut out an ear from thinly rolled paste and attach. Add decoration to disguise the join.

3 Mix the lustre dust with boiled water and paint fine gold detail on to the decorated elephants.

4 Place the royal icing in a piping bag fitted with a no 1 tube and pipe dots as desired. You are aiming for round balls of icing, not pointed cones, so adjust the consistency of your icing as necessary (see p28).

back to basics cookie recipes p14–17... sugarpaste p18... royal icing p20...

simply fantastic

These beautiful cookies were inspired by Japanese fans. It's surprisingly easy to paint on the delicate butterfly and blossom details with paste colours.

you will need...

- fan-shaped cookies
- sugarpaste: pale green, blue, pink, violet, light golden brown
- fan cookie cutters (lc)
- template p118
- cutting wheel
- palette knife
- craft knife
- micro embossers (hp: set 5)
- paste colours: pink, turquoise, mint green, violet, white
- fine brush

For the folds of the fan

1 Prepare the cookies as shown on p14–17. Roll out the sugarpaste in a colour of your choice and cut out a fan. Place one section of the fan template on to the paste, cut along the line with a cutting wheel and attach to the top half of the cookie.

2 Take the straight edge and, holding it at 60° to the cookie, repeatedly press it into the soft paste to make radial indentations to represent the folds. Trim away the right hand edge with a palette knife.

3 Use a craft knife to cut each folded section to a soft point at the top of the fan.

For the base of the fan

Thinly roll out light brown sugarpaste to 3mm (⅛in), cut to shape and attach to the base of the fan. Continue the radial lines on to this section with a palette knife. Emboss as desired and add a strip to the side and front of the fan.

Painting the fan

Mix the paste colours separately with cooled boiled water or clear alcohol. Stipple diluted paste in a darker shade over the folds, leaving a few windows of unpainted paste. Using a fine brush, paint dots of colour to represent blossom and butterflies.

back to basics   cookie recipes p14–17... sugarpaste p18...

funky owls

These designer owls combine bright, contemporary colours with bold patterns to create attractive cookies that will appeal to all ages.

you will need...

- owl-shaped cookies
- owl cookie cutter (lc)
- sugarpaste: brown, white, orange, three shades of blue
- piping gel
- cutters: 35mm & 45mm circle (fmm), scalloped diamond (lc), flower cutters eg flat florals (lc), large blossom (fmm)
- sugar glue
- no 18 piping tube (pme)
- cutting wheel

Decorating

For the body Roll out the brown sugarpaste and cut out a 45mm (⅕in) circle. Stick in position on the cookie using piping gel.

For the eyes Take the 35mm (⅛in) circle cutter and place in the position of one eye, cutting through the top of the brown paste and removing the excess. Repeat for the second eye. Cut 35mm (⅛in) circles from mid blue paste and stick in place with sugar glue.

For the eye decoration Thinly roll out the mid blue, brown and white pastes and cut out flowers and circles, using both ends of the piping tube. Attach to the cookie as shown. Add a folded over brown flower to the top of the cookie and cut off petals of an orange flower for feet.

For the wings Cut out the wing area from dark blue sugarpaste using the cookie cutter. Remove the body circle with the 45mm (⅕in) circle. Tidy up the shapes using a cutting wheel or craft knife and attach in place on the cookie.

For the beak Thinly roll out the orange paste and cut a 15mm (³⁄₁₆in) long scalloped diamond. Attach between the eyes, allowing the lower point to rise slightly so that the tip of the beak is slightly proud of the cookie.

back to basics cookie recipes p14–17... sugarpaste p18... sugar glue p23...

fabulously floral

Sugar flowers give cookies a 3D look that's as unexpected as it is beautiful. Either make the blooms yourself using simple sugarcrafting techniques, or buy them ready made and attach with a little sugar glue. A wide range of flowers can be achieved using moulds and you can use a sugar shaper fitted with a mesh disc for realistic centres. Experiment with eye-catching colour schemes, different cutters and tools to see how creative you can be.

Detailed leaves give a professional finish: try using a double sided leaf veiner (hp) for realistic effects.

thank you

... for your hospitality

There's nothing better than sharing a steaming hot cup of coffee with your friends. Return the favour by serving up this charming set of mugs.

you will need...

- ❀ mug-shaped cookies
- ❀ sugarpaste: white, pink, black
- ❀ mug cookie cutters (lc)
- ❀ piping gel
- ❀ flower cutter (lc: flat floral collection set 2)
- ❀ piping tube no. 18 (pme)
- ❀ craft knife

Trim strip decoration when in place on the cookie, using a craft knife

Covering

For the white mugs Prepare the cookies as shown on p14–17. Cut out mugs from white sugarpaste, using the cutter used to create the cookies. Cut away the handle area and a flattened disc from the top of the mugs and attach the body of the mug to the cookie using piping gel as glue.

For the pink mug Thinly roll out the pink paste, adding a little gum for firmness if desired, and cut out a mug shape. Remove the handle and a slightly larger flattened disc from the top of the mug, then attach to the cookie.

For the handles and top inside edge of mug Cut a mug shape from thinly rolled out white paste. Cut away the body of the mug, then take a craft knife and cut out the centre of the handle. Attach the handle on the cookie using piping gel. Create the top inside edge of the mug in the same way.

Decorating

Use a craft knife or sugarcraft cutters to cut white, pink or black sugarpaste to create your desired patterns, referring to the photo (right) for inspiration.

---

back to basics   cookie recipes p14–17... sugarpaste p18... pipng gel p22...

... for feeding the fish

Thank your neighbour for looking after your animals with these fun and quirky fish-shaped cookies.

you will need...

- ✿ fish-shaped cookies
- ✿ sugarpaste: orange, black, yellow
- ✿ fish cookie cutters (w)
- ✿ cutting wheel
- ✿ piping tube no. 16, 17 (pme)
- ✿ paste colours: orange yellow
- ✿ clear spirit e.g. gin, vodka

Covering

Prepare the cookies as shown on p14–17. Roll out the orange sugarpaste to 3mm (⅛in) and cut out fish shapes using the cookie cutter used to create the cookies.

Decorating

1 Take the cutting wheel and texture the fins and tail by repeatedly pulling the wheel towards and through the outside edge of the shape to create a feathered effect.

2 Mark the gills using a cutting wheel and attach to cookie.

3 Add the scales by repeatedly inserting a no. 16 piping tube, held at a 45° angle, into the soft paste.

4 For the eye, use a no. 17 piping tube to remove a circle of paste and replace with a ball of yellow paste to fit. For the pupil, roll a small ball of black paste and attach.

5 Dilute the suggested paste colours separately in clear spirit and paint over the texture of the cookies.

Create tropical fish by experimenting with different colours

back to basics cookie recipes p14–17... sugarpaste p18...

... for the gift

Say a big thank you for that special present with the sweet gift of a cookie. These pretty cookies make ideal favours for any birthday party or event.

you will need...

- ❀ gift-shaped cookies
- ❀ sugarpaste: dark brown, mid brown, pink, deep pink, violet, white
- ❀ gift cookie cutter (cg)
- ❀ circle cutters (fmm: geometric set)
- ❀ piping tubes no. 4, 16, 18 (pme)
- ❀ craft knife

Roll the paste for circles the same thickness by using narrow spacers

Covering

1 Prepare the cookies as shown on p14–17. Roll out the dark brown sugarpaste to 3mm (⅛in). Cut out the gift using the cutter used to create the cookies. Cut away the top section and attach the remainder to the cookie.

2 Thinly roll out sugarpaste in each colour, adding gum for firmness if desired, and cover with plastic to prevent drying.

Creating the concentric circles

1 Using a 4.5cm (1¾in) circle cutter, cut a circle from the deep pink paste.

2 Take the 3.5cm (1⅜in) circle cutter and centrally remove a circle from the larger circle. Replace this circle with a mid brown one and blend the join between the two circles by rubbing a finger over the pastes to smooth out any gaps.

3 Repeat with the 2.5cm (1in) circle and replace with a coffee coloured circle. Continue removing and replacing circles of different colours using the piping tubes as circle cutters. Attach to the cookie.

4 Make a selection of concentric circles in different sizes and colours, referring to the finished cookie photo for inspiration. Cut the circles to size once on the cookie using a craft knife.

5 Roll balls of deep pink paste to decorate the top of the gift and attach in place.

back to basics cookie recipes p14–17... sugarpaste p18...

... for your time

If a special someone has put aside some extra time for you recently, show your appreciation with these stylish art-deco inspired clock face cookies.

you will need...

- round cookies
- sugarpaste: red, silver, coral pink, black
- round cookie/pastry cutters
- circle cutters (fmm: geometric set)
- piping tubes no. 4, 16, 18 (pme)
- cutting wheel

Use a soft paintbrush to remove cut circles from piping tubes

Covering

1 Prepare the cookies as shown on p14–17. Roll out red, silver and coral pink sugarpaste to 3mm (1/8in).

2 Use a 4.5cm (1 4/5in) cutter to cut a circle from red paste. Carefully remove the excess paste from around the cutter to prevent the sugarpaste distorting. Take a 3.5cm (1 2/5in) circle cutter and centrally remove a circle from the larger circle.

3 Replace this circle with a silver one and blend the join between the two circles by rubbing a finger over the pastes to smooth out any gaps. Repeat with a 2.5cm (1in) circle cutter on the silver circle and replace with a coral pink one, smoothing gaps. Attach the concentric circle to the centre of the cookie.

4 Use a no. 18 piping tube to cut four circles of each colour and attach to represent the hours. Cut the clock hands freehand from black paste using a cutting wheel and attach in position.

back to basics cookie recipes p14–17... sugarpaste p18...

thanks a bunch

What better way to say thank you than with this floral centrepiece? Use a striking single colour or experiment with coloured sugarpaste for a blossoming display.

you will need...

- 🌸 floral shaped cookies
- 🌸 cookie sticks
- 🌸 sugarpaste: red, orange, brown
- 🌸 nesting blossom cookie cutters (w)
- 🌸 daisy centre stamps
- 🌸 cutting wheel
- 🌸 ball tool
- 🌸 florist staysoft, oasis or polystyrene

Use a sugar shaper to make an alternative flower centre

Baking

Prepare the cookies as shown on p14–17, bake and insert a cookie stick into each cookie immediately as they come out of the oven, before they cool and harden.

Covering the red flower

Roll out the red sugarpaste to 3mm (⅛in) and cut out the floral shapes using the nesting blossom cookie cutters. Take the cutting wheel and cut through the petals to separate. Place a petal in the palm of your hand and run a ball tool around the edges to thin and shape. Repeat for the remaining petals. Attach to the cookie, slightly overlapping each petal with the previous one. Use a daisy centre stamp to create a brown centre for each cookie.

Creating the centrepiece

Place some florist Staysoft, Oasis or polystyrene into a suitable container and cover the top as you wish. Arrange the sticks in a container, wrap cellophane around the outside and secure to make a perfect gift.

back to basics cookie recipes p14–17... sugarpaste p18...

sweet dreams

Those with a sweet tooth won't be able to resist these treats! Use bright colours and bold patterns and experiment with a variety of cutters to recreate your favourite candies in cookie form. I've added lollypop sticks and cellophane wrapping for an impressive finishing touch. A great addition to any party, although watch out – they won't be around for long!

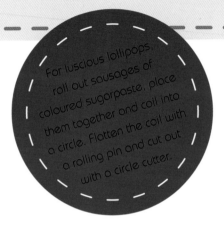

For luscious lollipops, roll out sausages of coloured sugarpaste, place them together and coil into a circle. Flatten the coil with a rolling pin and cut out with a circle cutter.

striking stockings

These super stockings look wonderful hanging from the Christmas tree. I've given instructions for the snowman design, but you can use the same techniques for a range of festive patterns.

you will need...

- ❁ stocking-shaped cookies
- ❁ piping tube no. 18 (pme)
- ❁ sugarpaste: black, white, red, green, orange
- ❁ stocking cookie cutters
- ❁ royal icing
- ❁ cutters: star (lc) snowman (pc: christmas midi set)
- ❁ piping bag

Baking

Prepare the cookies as shown on p14–17. Remove a small circle of dough from the top of the cookie using the piping tube and bake.

Covering

Roll out the green and red paste to 3mm (⅛in). Cut out a stocking from each colour using the cutter. Cut across the top of each stocking and attach the red body and green top to the cookie. Remove a circle from the green top to reveal the hole.

Decorating

1 Thinly roll out the white, black and green sugarpastes, adding gum for firmness as desired (see p19).

2 Emboss snowmen into each colour of paste and use a craft knife to cut along the embossed lines of the shapes. Attach the appropriate sections of paste to the cookie and trim to fit. Add an orange nose. Make the tree and attach, then decorate with stars and baubles

3 Pipe a row of royal iced dots on to the green stocking top and the tree.

back to basics cookie recipes p14–17... sugarpaste p18... royal icing p20...

gingerbread family

Children will simply adore this gingerbread family and snow-topped house, and they're lots of fun to create too!

you will need...

- ❀ gingerbread family and house cookies
- ❀ sugarpaste: red
- ❀ mini quilting embosser (pc)
- ❀ gingerbread family and house cookie cutters
- ❀ cutting wheel
- ❀ piping gel
- ❀ piping bag
- ❀ piping tube no. 1.5, 3 (pme)
- ❀ royal icing

Covering

Prepare the cookies as shown on p17. Roll out red sugarpaste to 3mm (⅛in). Emboss with the mini quilter, taking care to line it up each time you need to repeat the embossing.

Decorating

1 Cut out a gingerbread man using the cookie cutter used to create the cookies. Take the cutting wheel and cut a waistcoat shape using the shape of the gingerbread man as a guide. Attach to the cookie using piping gel. Repeat for the children, altering the shape of their clothing, and for the door of the house, using the photo (right) as a guide.

2 Fill a piping bag with royal icing and attach the no. 1.5 piping tube. Pipe around the outline of the cookies then add buttons, facial features and details. Use the no. 3 tube to add snow to the house.

Check the icing's consistency before you start piping

back to basics   gingerbread p17... sugarpaste p18... royal icing p20...

crackers about you

These cracking cookies will make a great table decoration on Christmas Day and provide a delicious gift to your guests as well.

you will need...

- cracker-shaped cookies (lc)
- craft knife
- sugarpaste: gold, red, burgundy
- cracker cookie cutters (lc)
- cutting wheel
- dresden tool
- edible gold lustre dust (sk)
- confectioners' glaze
- piping tube no. 16, 18 (pme)
- small circle cutter

Baking

Prepare the cookies as shown on p14–17. To make the pulled cracker, cut a zigzag line through the central section of a dough cracker, using a craft knife. Separate the two halves and bake.

Covering

1 Cover each cracker with gold sugarpaste. For the pulled cracker, place the sugarpaste on the cookie and trim the zigzag section to shape using a craft knife.

2 Use a cutting wheel to mark four curved outside edges of the gathered sections on each cookie. Indent radial gathers using a Dresden tool.

3 Mix edible gold lustre dust with confectioners' glaze and paint over the gold sugarpaste to add extra sparkle. Allow to dry.

4 Thinly roll out the red and burgundy pastes, adding gum for firmness if desired. Using the craft knife, cut thin strips of paste and attach to the centre of the gathered sections. Shape bows or ties, as desired.

5 Cut circles of paste using the cutter and piping tubes and attach to the crackers in patterns of your choice.

back to basics cookie recipes p14–17... sugarpaste p18... confectioners' glaze p22...

brilliant baubles

The combination of striking colours with sparkling disco dust makes these baubles such festive decorations – they're better than the real thing!

you will need...

- christmas bauble cookies
- sugarpaste: a selection of colours
- christmas bauble cookie cutters
- piping gel
- royal icing
- piping bag and no. 2, 18 tube (pme)
- edible snowflake lustre dust (sk)
- white hologram disco dust (ea)
- soft brush

Baking

Prepare the cookies as shown on p14–17. Remove a small circle of dough from the top of the cookies using a piping tube and bake.

Covering

Roll out the coloured sugarpaste and cut a bauble using the cookie cutter used to create the cookies. Attach to the cookie using piping gel and remove a circle using the no. 18 tube to reveal the hole in the cookie.

Decorating

For the purple bauble Fill a piping bag with royal icing, attach the no. 2 tube and pipe a swirl and coil pattern over the cookie. Once the royal icing has set, mix some lustre dust with water and paint over the pattern. Use a soft brush to spread white hologram dust over the cookie.

Use the photo (right) for further inspiration on how to decorate each bauble

back to basics   cookie recipes p14–17... sugarpaste p18... royal icing p20...

snowflake centrepiece

These elegant snowflakes make an attractive centrepiece, or would look great hanging from your tree. Remember, every snowflake should be different!

you will need...

- cookie dough
- snowflake cookie cutters
- royal icing
- piping bag
- piping bag and no 1.5, 18 tube (pme)
- silver sugar balls: 4mm (⅛in), 6mm (¾₀in), 8mm (⅜in)
- white vegetable fat
- edible white hologram dust (ea)

Creating the snowflakes

Cut out snowflake shapes from the cookie dough. Using the small cutters and the no. 18 piping tube, remove geometric shapes from inside each snowflake. Remove a small circle of dough from the top of the cookies using a piping tube and bake as shown on p12–13.

Decorating the snowflakes

Fill a piping bag fitted with a 1.5 tube with royal icing. Pipe lines and dots over the cookies and secure silver balls in place with a dot of royal icing. Once the icing has dried, paint white vegetable fat over all the decoration and sprinkle with white hologram dust. Tie silver cord, ribbon or elastic to a selection of your snowflake cookies and hang as desired.

Add silver balls at the last minute to avoid them tarnishing in damp or humid conditions

back to basics   cookie recipes p14–17... royal icing p20...

heaven sent

Bake these cookies for your own little angels this Christmas. So simple to create, I used a star cutter (w) to cut out the star cookies and added sugarpaste in a variety of colours. The angels are cut from angel cutters (cg) and covered in blue, gold and cream sugarpaste. You may find a Dresden tool handy for adding texture to the wings, by flicking up small sections of sugarpaste with the pointed end, or adding detail to the dresses. The angels' hair can be created by using a sugar shaper fitted with a mesh disc. They are simply divine!

Use a piping tube to cut small holes in the cookies when baking, then add gold and silver ribbons and hang them from your Christmas tree.

templates

To use the templates,
trace over the image onto
greaseproof paper or white
paper and then transfer it onto card.
Cut around the traced outline of the
card to produce your template. All
templates are shown at full size.

Indian elephant (p84)

Bride and groom (p38)

Groom

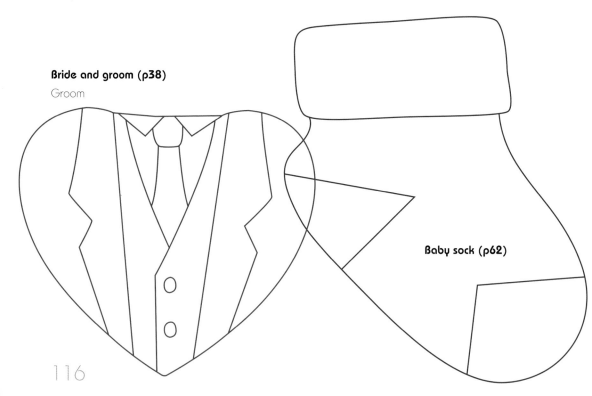

Baby sock (p62)

116

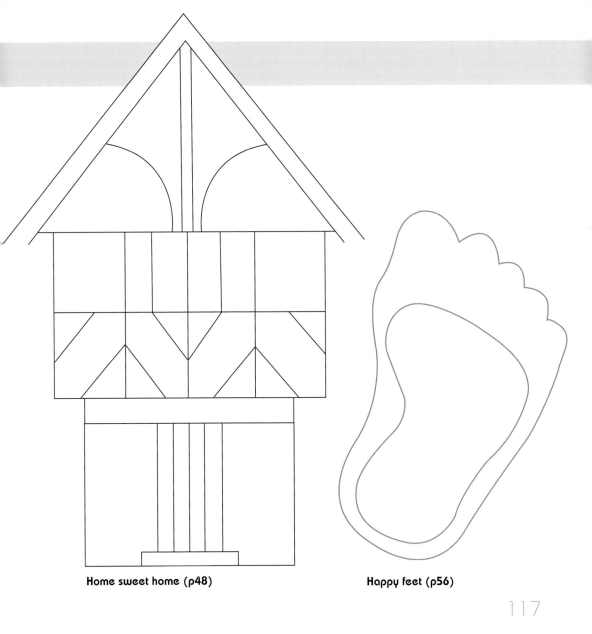

Home sweet home (p48)

Happy feet (p56)

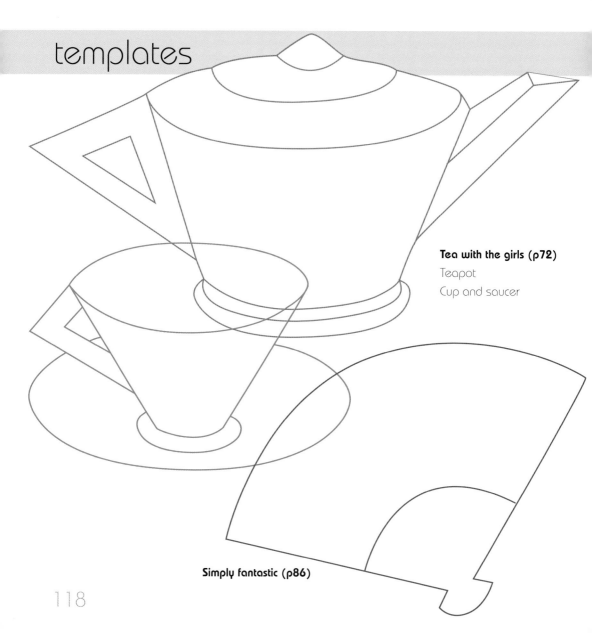

Tea with the girls (p72)
Teapot
Cup and saucer

Simply fantastic (p86)

acknowledgments

I'd like to thank Sally for her enthusiasm and for introducing me to her gingerbread men. Thanks to Raymond and Beth Braman of www.coppergifts.com for sending me samples of their copper cookie cutters. Discovering the range and sizes of cutters was quite a revelation! A special thank you also to Pat of Knightbridge PME, for supplying a selection of Wilton cookie cutters, I found the nesting sets really useful.

about the author

Lindy Smith is a world-renowned designer, author and teacher and author of five cake-decorating titles for D&C: **Creative Celebration Cakes, Storybook Cakes, Celebrate with a Cake!, Party Animal Cakes** and **Cakes to Inspire and Desire.**

Lindy loves nothing better than sharing her love of sugarcraft with fellow enthusiasts from all over the world, via workshops and demonstrations. She has also appeared on television in programmes such as **The Generation Game** and presented a sugarcraft series on **Good Food Live.**

Lindy also manages Lindy's Cakes, a well established business that runs **www.lindyscakes.co.uk** for the online shop, sugarcraft and cake decorating shows and workshops both in the UK and abroad.

suppliers

UK

Lindy's Cakes Ltd (LC)
Unit 2, Station Approach
Wendover, Aylesbury
Bucks, HP22 6BN
Tel: +44(0)1296 623906
www.lindyscakes.co.uk
*Manufacturer of stainless steel
cookie and sugarcraft cutters plus
mail order equipment supplies as
used in Lindy's books.*

Knightbridge PME Ltd (W)
Chadwell Heath Lane
Romford
Essex RN6 4NP
Tel: +44 (0)208 590 5959
www.cakedecoration.co.uk
*Sugarcraft and cookies cutter
supplier and UK distributor of
Wilton products.*

Abbreviations used in this book:

CG	CopperGifts
EA	Edible Art
FMM	FMM Sugarcraft
HP	Holly Products
JEM	JEM Cutters c.c.
LC	Lindy's Cakes Ltd
PC	Patchwork Cutters
PME	PME Sugarcraft
SK	Squires Kitchen
W	Wilton

US

Global Sugar Art
7 Plattsburgh Plaza
Plattsburgh, NY 12901
Tel: 518-561-3039
www.globalsugarart.com
*Sugarcraft supplier that imports
many UK products to the US.*

CopperGifts.com (CG)
900 N. 32nd St
Parsons, KS 67357
Tel: 620.421.0654
www.Coppergifts.com
*Supplier of handmade copper
cookie cutters, in over 1000
designs.*

Wilton Industries, Inc. (W)
2240 West 75th Street
Woodridge, 1L 60517
United States
Tel: (Retail Customer orders):
+1 800 794 5866
www.wilton.com
*Industry leader in celebration,
crafts and specialty
housewares.*

index